# ' O SHIPS' FIGUREHEAD COLLECTION

*The National Maritime Museum at Greenwich is the national museum of the Royal Navy and the merchant shipping industry and celebrates most other aspects of man's encounter with the sea.*

*Apart from its galleries at Greenwich the Museum maintains several small outstations in the West Country, in conjunction with other organisations who own and run the premises in which these 'detached displays' are situated; the Museum's 'Valhalla' Figurehead Collection is one such.*

*This account of 'Valhalla' is intended both for visitors to Tresco and for others interested in figureheads but who may not be able to visit the Collection. It is the first of a number of such booklets which the Museum hopes to publish on its outstations and succeeds that issued by the Tresco Estate in 1972.*

*Various members of the Museum, and others, have contributed to the new text which has been prepared by John Stengelhofen, the Museum's Curator in the West Country. He has also designed and in part illustrated the work, which has been produced in Cornwall under his supervision.*

The figureheads in the Valhalla Collection represent the final century in a tradition dating back over three thousand years. From earliest times ships' bows have carried carvings of human or animal forms as part of the overall decoration of the vessels, although the motives and meanings behind these often elaborate figures have altered over the centuries. Their pattern, size and shape have also adapted to fit new types of ships' hull, while the artistic style of figureheads and other decoration has changed to reflect contemporary fashions.

At 'Valhalla' most of the 28 figureheads date from the middle and end of the 19th century and come from merchant sailing vessels or early steamships that were wrecked on the Isles of Scilly. As such the collection is a random cross-section from generally modest vessels, whose small and simple figureheads contrast with larger naval examples which survive elsewhere, such as the National Maritime Museum at Greenwich. At 'Valhalla' one sees more of the popular skills of the Victorian carver of fairground figures, shop and inn signs, rather than of the formal heraldic sculpture which adorned ships-of-the-line.

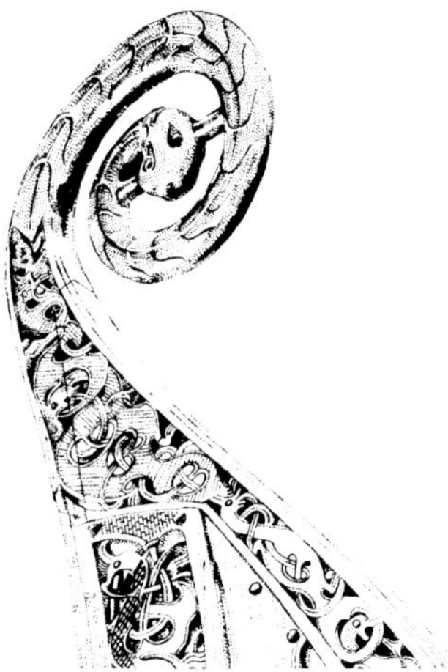

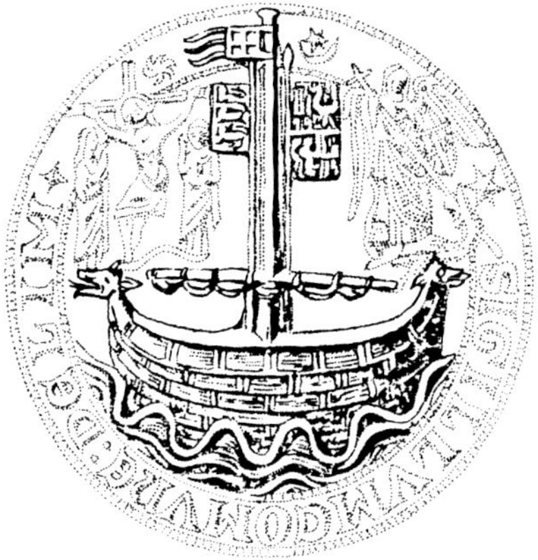

Left to right:
Serpent prow of the Oseberg ship, early 9th century, in the Viking Ships Museum, Oslo.
HMS *Ajax*, 74 guns, built 1809; a fine Royal Naval figurehead.
Ship on the seal of Lyme Regis, Dorset, 1284 (after Ewe, 1972).

The standard of each piece also varies; some are almost crude caricatures, others have smooth lines and flowing robes which are very much in the classic tradition.

The figurehead remained the principal feature of the decoration applied to sailing ships over the centuries and it was only reluctantly given up after fifty years of steamship development showed it to be impractical. In the sailing ship it had become a tradition; a feature of the design of all but the smallest vessels and a part of maritime folklore. Seamen — naturally cautious, conservative and superstitious — did all they could to maintain the tradition; they expected a figurehead and were suspicious if it was not there.

The origin of the figurehead is complex but its development, independently in different places, indicates a universal instinct among seafarers to protect themselves from the evil spirits of the deep, to placate the gods, or to put fear into an enemy. It also acknowledges the personality of the vessel, as does the related and recurring "eye" motif on ships' bows, which supposedly allows the vessel mystically to avoid hazards ahead. In recent centuries it has, in fighting ships, symbolised the prestige and power of the king and country. There were also less magical reasons for figureheads, which by their position on the bow form the natural decorative climax to the rising sheer of a sailing vessel and give scope for man's urge to embellish even the most functional objects. Similarly, they were a means of ship identification and gave the owner a chance to honour heroes of the period or commemorate himself or a member of his family.

## Development

Among the earliest examples of figureheads is that represented on an alabaster model boat from the tomb of the Pharaoh Tutankhamun, where the upwards sweep of the bow takes the form of an ibex, a wild goat. The Oseberg Viking ship, excavated in Norway, shows intricate carving culminating in a curving snake's head at the prow and similar beast and dragon figures in the same tradition appear on the 11th century Bayeux tapestry. The prominent "eye" motif on the bows of vessels was found in ancient Egypt, China, Phoenicia, Greece and Rome and survives to this day on Portuguese and other traditional fishing boats.

Evidence on early figureheads is sparse but shows some idea of what was expected. Actual examples are rare and, apart from those found in Norse ship graves, most evidence comes from drawings, coins, models and the heraldic representation of ships on the seals of maritime towns. All these, small in scale, give us little detail and it is not until the 18th century that we can begin to have an idea of the actual form of figureheads or can assess the competence and style of the carvers. The occasional drawing from the 15th and 16th centuries and then, in the 17th and 18th centuries, the more detailed shipwrights' draughts and models, especially those made in Britain for the Navy Board, show the progression of ship design and the resulting changes in figureheads.

The gargoyle-like Gothic figure, tucked under a cumbersome fore-castle in the 15th century, becomes a prominent feature on the end of a low beak in the next century — often an upright standing figure or one mounted on horseback. The 17th century growth in European naval power brought with it flamboyant baroque decoration, at times reaching the impractical proportions which prompted one French captain to saw off part of his figurehead on leaving port! King Charles I's *Sovereign of the Seas* of 1637 cost £40,000 to build, of which no less than £7,000 was spent on the gilded decorative carving, including a figure of King Edgar on horseback. The lion became a common figurehead for Royal Naval vessels, especially smaller ones, as the Navy Board attempted to reduce the cost of elaborate carvings. More restrained, classical architectural motifs and the use of paint rather than gold leaf also reduced expense. Sailors, shipwrights and officers still contrived to ignore the Admiralty orders but by 1796 the regulations only permitted carved scrolls — fiddle or billet-heads (see p. 11) — except in first-rate ships. The tradition continued in the early ironclads, such as HMS *Warrior* of 1860 with its massive half figure, but an order of 1894 finally abolished all figureheads in the Royal Navy.

The big merchant ships of the 17th and 18th centuries, heavily armed and almost indistinguishable from naval vessels, had similar figureheads and decorations. Smaller merchant ships could be equally elaborate and all but the smallest sailing boats and barges would carry some carved decoration. The vast increase in trade following the Industrial Revolution was reflected in a boom period for shipbuilding. Builders' yards up and down the country were kept busy on vessels of all types for all trades, coastal and foreign. Specialist "ships' carvers" set up in business in all the major shipbuilding centres but no doubt in the smaller yards — such as in the West Country — one of the more skilled shipwrights would have been given the task of carving the one or two figureheads which might be needed each year.

The standard of materials, furnishings and decorations in all these vessels depended on the trade for which they were intended and its anticipated profitability. The large China tea-clippers, such as *Friar Tuck* (see no. 27), would have finely carved figures while, at the other extreme, something very rough or modest might suffice for a small coastal craft. Brigs in the

Bow of the 1869 clipper *Cutty Sark* at Greenwich, showing a typical arrangement of figurehead and trail boards with the ship's name. The figurehead represents the witch Nannie, from Burns' poem *Tam O'Shanter*.

Newcastle to London coal trade, for example, did without any decoration of the stem-post, the cost-conscious owners being unwilling or unable to pay for such luxuries. During the 1840s the shape of large ships' bows began to change from the near vertical with a figure almost standing upright, to the raked clipper bow of the last "tall ships". This ultimate development in sailing vessels led to the adoption of near horizontal figureheads and decorative trail boards, setting off the clean, simple lines of the hull. This fashion perhaps appeals more to us today than the earlier excesses of baroque carving. At any rate, the disappearance of large commercial sailing ships in the 1930s, took with it the profession of figurehead and ship's carver although some figurehead carving is still done, largely in connection with ship restoration projects. It is also worth looking at the bows of modern ships, where there is often a company badge or other decoration, a vestige of the figurehead tradition.

# SCILLY AND THE SEA

The Isles of Scilly lie in a commanding position twenty-eight miles off Land's End, the south-west corner of mainland Britain. Low-lying and spread over ten miles of sea, their innumerable granite outcrops and islets, together with the six inhabited islands, form a major hazard to shipping entering the English Channel or rounding Land's End for the Bristol Channel and the Irish Sea. This position has inevitably resulted in countless wrecks and drownings around the Islands, yet in the days of sail they were also ideally sited as a base for pilots and for many other maritime activities — legal and illegal. The sea is the major

Lion figurehead of a Royal Naval sixth-rate, c.1670, in the National Maritime Museum, Greenwich. Once the commonest pattern, only two such lions now survive; the other one is built into the Red Lion Inn at Martlesham, Suffolk.

HMS *Hogue,* 74 guns, built 1811; a late example of a Royal Naval lion figurehead in the National Maritime Museum, Greenwich.

influence on the life of all island people and particularly so on the Scillies, which from prehistoric times were remote and impoverished. Fishing and farming the poor land were traditional occupations from early times but neither were adequate to support a growing population, who turned their isolation to advantage in other ways.

The Islands became a base for piracy on a large scale. Loaded merchantmen, inward bound after months at sea, proved easy meat for predators lurking among the Islands, at a time when those in authority locally could also indulge in such activities with little risk of punishment. Piracy became so extensive that in 1209 the Priory of Tresco beheaded no fewer than 112 pirates! After 1549, when the administrator of the Islands, Lord Seymour, was himself beheaded for piracy and acts against the Crown, the Scillies were garrisoned and attempts were made to impose the rule of law under a new system of Governors.

Wrecking — in the sense of stealing cargo from vessels lost by accident — was another activity. Indeed, so great were the number of wrecks that the islanders could almost consider this a regular source of many luxuries and some essentials, otherwise unobtainable, as well as a useful supply of building timber and fuel on the sparsely wooded Islands. Despite the erection of the first lighthouse on St Agnes in 1680, the number of wrecks only diminished with the advent of steamships. More powerful lights and modern navigational aids have now substantially reduced but not eliminated wrecks and, just as on mainland Cornwall, it would have been considered wasteful not to make use of this rich bounty, brought in by almost every storm. It compensated, in part, for the hard living conditions which the self-same sea imposed on the islanders. The oft-quoted prayer, attributed among others to the Rev. John Troutbeck of Scilly, illustrated one attitude to such activities: "Dear God, we pray not that wrecks should happen but if it be Thy will that they do, we pray Thee let them be to the benefit of Thy poor people of Scilly". There is no good evidence for traditions that the Scillonians did more than just pray to encourage wrecks but the suspicion of deliberate wrecking must always remain. In 1681 the keeper of St Agnes' lighthouse took away part of a cargo, having apparently failed to light his coal-fired beacon until after a Virginian trader had struck the rocks. The Brethren of Trinity House, who had preferred to appoint an outsider, were surprised "that one who had gone to live at Scilly would in three months become a wrecker". (The original cresset from the St Agnes light has been preserved and can be seen in the Tresco Gardens).

Smuggling, like wrecking, can hardly be claimed an exclusively Scillonian activity but both flourished more than elsewhere due to the Islands' ideal position. They were remote but within easy reach of the Channel Islands and the coast of France. Also they were a landfall for ships returning from all over the world and needing fresh food, water and a Channel pilot for the last stage of their journey.

Some "free-trading", unencumbered by tedious customs and excise regulations, was understandable — the islanders would supply a bucket of much-needed potatoes for a bucket of tea — but it was tobacco, wine and spirits that formed the real foundation of the business.

Cottages at Old Grimsby, Tresco. Long since demolished, they were described as "smugglers' cottages" when photographed in 1880 by Alexander Gibson.

Fishing boats, pilot cutters and gigs, as well as larger vessels, brought illicit "duty-free" goods to the Islands for redistribution to all parts of the south-west and beyond — when the destination was reported free of preventive officers! People at all levels of society were involved (since the larger ventures required capital and organisation) and even the poor Rev. Troutbeck was forced to resign his living on the Islands in disgrace, in 1795, through his contraband transactions.

The light, fast, six-oared pilot gigs, still to be seen on the Islands, were restricted to a crew of four to prevent their being rowed across the Channel, while the profitable illegal trade almost unavoidably led to violence. In 1791 two customs boatmen were shot dead off Old Grimsby, Tresco, while attempting to apprehend the *Friendship*. Her owner, James Dunkin, was found guilty of murder in his absence, the Board of Customs offering a £500 reward. Records of minor incidents abound during the 18th century; scuffles on dark beaches, chases at sea with fast revenue cutters, the boarding of ships and the seizure of contraband goods — or the escape — as well as the final, curiously lenient view of such misdemeanours taken by the local magistrates. This leniency probably owed less to criminal sympathies from the Bench than to the knowledge that, for most islanders, successful smuggling provided occasional relief from abject poverty. Smuggling on a large scale was eliminated by about 1800, thus ending the more unsavoury aspects of the Islands' maritime history.

Against this colourful record must be set a more positive and equally skilful one, the long and remarkable history of Scillonians as pilots — helping others to avoid the loss of lives and vessels —

Burying the victims of the SS *Schiller* disaster, 1875, (see p.28). Over 300 people died — more than in any local wreck apart from that of the *Association* and her consorts in 1707.

New Grimsby harbour today and the channel between Tresco and Bryher.

The last vessel to be built on Porthcressa, St Mary's, the *David Auterson,* launched in 1871.

as lifeboat crews and in the unofficial lifesaving exploits of the pilot gigs.

The pilots, traditionally from St Agnes, had an intimate knowledge both of the Islands and much of the coast of southern Britain. Setting off in their gigs or small cutters in any weather to meet and offer their services to an approaching vessel, the Scillonian pilots were held in high regard for their skill and reliability. Their gigs' excellent handling in heavy seas meant that both before and after the introduction of the first lifeboat on St Mary's in 1837, they performed many outstanding rescues. Although a lifeboat was also stationed on St Agnes from 1890 it was not until the arrival of a motor lifeboat on St Mary's in 1919 that the official service was able to cover all the Islands. As in the rest of Britain that service is still manned by local volunteers — in Scilly's case the present generation of her skilled seamen and fishermen.

Augustus Smith surrounded by a group of St Agnes pilots, 1871.

## AUGUSTUS SMITH AND 'VALHALLA'

The early years of the 19th century saw an unprecedented level of poverty on the Islands. In 1811, Trinity House reduced the number of licensed pilots, and the price of kelp (the ash produced by burning seaweed of the same name to produce soda for glass making) had dropped to an uneconomic level. Petitions for help were sent to the mainland and finally, in 1831, the Duke of Leeds gave up his lease of the Islands after a family connection of some 260 years.

The arrival of Augustus Smith, who was to begin the Valhalla Collection of figureheads, was a turning point in the modern history of Scilly. Smith's lease of the Islands from 1834 until his death, ended centuries of quasi-military rule from the garrison and absentee Governors, as well as the more precarious economic aspects of the population's existence.

A landowner from Hertfordshire, Smith held his lease from the Duchy of Cornwall and moved to the Islands with the express purpose of improving the lot of the people. With advanced ideas, the "Lord Proprietor" as he became known, set about reforming many aspects of Island life, encouraging industries such as shipbuilding and fishing, introducing compulsory education thirty years ahead of the mainland and creating larger and more economic farms by discouraging subdivision of land among families. He ensured a regular postal service and himself financed many building operations for the benefit of the islanders. Some of his actions, such as promoting emigration of the unemployed to the mainland, resulted in criticism but overall he was a benevolent dictator whose 38-year rule transformed the Islands. He and his successors created a basis for their prosperity, which has been further transformed in recent years by visitors and tourism. Among Smith's building projects, in part designed to relieve unemployment, was a residence for himself on Tresco. He chose a sheltered site on the southern end of the island, near where a small monastic cell had been established by King Athelstan in AD 927. Of this, nothing but some ruined walls remained and the name by which the new house has always been known — The Abbey. In 1838 he moved into his new home, which though away from St Mary's was reasonably central for all the other Islands. By 19th century standards the original house was of modest size — even for a bachelor like Smith — and later extensions including the tower were added by his successor, who had a large family.

Tresco Abbey, about 1890.

The original plans included a large area of terraced gardens and here Smith and his descendants established the present Tropical Gardens. Plants and trees from every continent were obtained and many Scillonian sailors returned from distant voyages with cuttings for the Lord Proprietor. At an early date Smith started to collect figureheads and other "mementoes" of the numerous wrecks around the islands. Probably the earliest to contribute to the collection occurred three years after he came to the Abbey when the *Thames,* the Dublin-London steam packet (see no. 59), went onto the Western Rocks with the loss of all but four on board. For several years the collection stood on the terrace outside the Abbey but later, in laying out the south-west corner of the gardens, Smith included a small open loggia building beside his new bowling green, to house his fast-growing museum. About 1870 he acquired some two tons of seashells from German sailors whose ships were sheltering in the road-steads during the Franco-Prussian War — "for I know not what, till some purpose may suggest itself for them". These shells were used to decorate the original 'Valhalla' building, as can still be seen.

While on one of his frequent visits to the mainland, in 1872, Augustus Smith fell ill and died in Plymouth, aged 68 years. He left instructions for his burial at St Buryan near Land's End, where the prominent church tower is clearly visible from the Islands with a telescope.

Augustus Smith (1806–72); a photograph taken about 1870.

Two years later, after resigning his army commission, Augustus' 26-year-old nephew and heir, Lt. Algernon Dorrien-Smith, arrived to take up residence at the Abbey and continue the family tradition. He was also a benevolent squire and "Lord Proprietor" for nearly half a century, continuing to develop the Gardens and adding to the figurehead collection, as well as establishing the famous Scillonian flower-growing industry. One of his daughters, Charlotte (born 1877) also compiled the first comprehensive list of wrecks around the Islands.

Three generations on, the Dorrien-Smith family still live at the Abbey, though now only holding the island of Tresco on a lease from the Duchy of Cornwall.

The Valhalla Collection was formally acquired by the National Maritime Museum in 1979 as part of the tax settlement following the death of Lt-Cmdr. Thomas Dorrien-Smith. The collection is maintained by the Museum and is administered as one of its West Country Outstations in partnership with the Tresco Estate.

# CONSERVATION

Visitors to 'Valhalla' have occasionally commented that the figureheads look "too new" and have queried the policy of restoring the carvings in the collection, many of which were literally washed up on the beach as fragments of wreckage.

If the collection had been housed in a modern, air-conditioned building, the decisions on restoration policy would indeed have been difficult as the options would have been numerous. At 'Valhalla' conditions for the figureheads are similar to those they would have known when mounted on a ship's bow, though without the extremes encountered at sea. The atmosphere is damp and salt-laden but with warm winters and no pounding from heavy seas. Policy for the restoration, commenced in 1957 by Mr H R Allen, was largely dictated by these circumstances.

Lt-Cmdr. Dorrien-Smith's decision at that time to extend the museum building in the same style as the original, to accommodate the numerous exhibits added since Augustus

*Rosa Tacchini* (no. 56); an unrestored figurehead.
Figurehead conservation at 'Valhalla'.

Smith first built his 'Valhalla', was in itself an act of conservation. It maintained the historical link between the figureheads, the environment in which they were wrecked and the 19th century concept of their display. The original ceiling was undulating, to suggest that the spectator was walking under the waves and was set with thousands of granite chippings which glittered from above. The walls were lined with large seashells to enhance the atmosphere. Once the plan for the building and display had been established the manner of restoration developed from it. Most of the damage caused to the carvings over a hundred years or more, was from a combination of drying, shrinking and splitting, which in their turn let in rain water. Rot ensued and many of the carvings were actually or nearly falling apart when work was started. Rainwater is far more damaging than salt water, which has preservative qualities and probably kept the timber at a more constant humidity when the figureheads were at sea.

There were two other problems. On the one hand, the surface condition of most of the carvings was too worn and porous to protect them against weather; on the other, a few had been so plastered with paint, voyage after voyage and often very crudely, that while protected, all trace of their carved detail had been buried. The *Rosherville* figurehead (no. 44), for example, had big black moustaches modelled entirely in paint! In all cases the aim was to bring each item as nearly as possible to its original condition as fitted to its ship — painted and varnished to the best traditional standard and also protected against further weather damage.

With this in mind every piece of carving was carefully stripped down to the original wood, note kept of the colour scheme first used, the use of gold leaf and the style of painting where it was possible to judge this. Two of the carvings appeared to have been wrecked on their maiden voyage, or after a refit, and some areas of the original paintwork remained to show how subtly they had been treated, in keeping with the portrait-like quality of the best pieces. No repair of carving or restoration of paint was undertaken without substantial evidence. For example, when an arm had been broken off without any indication of its pose, it was not replaced. On the other hand, where an area of surface carving was found rotten it was duplicated in sound timber. The result of this policy is that the visitor sees a collection which, while varied, is both aesthetically consistent with its origins and well protected.

At the time of writing some figureheads have been temporarily removed from display for major repair. With a continuing programme of maintenance, other pieces will occasionally be removed to allow further work to be carried out. This is a considerable and expensive commitment, given the specialised nature of the work and the fact that in the conditions of Tresco, paintwork will only last about twenty-five or thirty years, let alone any other repair which may be needed.

# Acknowledgements

The Museum wishes to thank the following for their kind assistance: Richard Larn, whose researches into West Country shipwrecks have proved an invaluable source of information; Frank Gibson, who as fourth generation photographer on St Mary's has provided the historic wreck photographs and other Island views; Robert Dorrien-Smith and the Tresco Estate; Simon Smith, now in charge of conservation work on the Collection, who has provided notes on this topic. The colour photographs were taken by Marie Richardson and John Stengelhofen, of the Museum, and by Simon Smith; other historic photographs are from the collection of the Royal Institution of Cornwall.

The following publications have been particularly useful in compiling this account:

*Shipwrecks Around the Isles of Scilly* (Isles of Scilly Museum Publication no. 3, rev. ed., 1980); based on Charlotte Dorrien-Smith's list (1953).

Elisabeth Inglis-Jones, *Augustus Smith of Scilly* (Faber, 1969).

Richard Larn, *Cornish Shipwrecks* [*vol. III*] *The Isles of Scilly* (David and Charles, 1971).

Clive Mumford, *Portrait of the Isles of Scilly* (Robert Hale, 1967).

Peter Norton, *Figureheads* (HMSO/National Maritime Museum, 1972).

M K Stammers, *Ships' Figureheads* (Shire Publications, 1983).

A number of exhibits cannot so far be matched with any likely ship. In some cases no records have been found, in others it may be that they were simply washed ashore as unidentifiable flotsam. Accounts of shipwrecks also tend to vary and though efforts at accuracy have been made the National Maritime Museum would be grateful for any amendment which would improve its records and future editions of this booklet.

Details of ships, where known, are given at the end of each entry as follows:

***Name of vessel:*** rig/propulsion, tonnage* **R**: Port of registry at loss
**B**: Builder/place of building, date **D**: Registered dimensions†
**O**: Owner at loss **M**: Master at loss
**V**: Voyage **C**: Cargo **W**: Date of wreck/loss

*registered or gross. †length×beam×depth in hold in feet and tenths.

1.

Technical terms:

*Fiddle-head:* A carved scroll, used instead of a figurehead, turning upwards and aft in the manner of a violin, hence the name.

*Billet-head:* A carved scroll used as above but turning forwards and down; also called a scroll head.

*Trail boards:* Carved or painted boards on each side of the stem of a vessel stretching back from the figurehead for decorative effect; they often carry the vessel's name.

# THE COLLECTION

## AWARD 1

One of the carved blue and gold trail boards from the *Award* which was re-lettered to form a sign for the Valhalla Collection. Carved letters screwed to the surface of the board had been used for the ship's name; all these were missing but their shape was visible on the old paintwork, so their exact form could be reproduced. The other half of the pair has also been altered to form the signboard for the New Inn, the island's "pub".

The *Award* was wrecked on Gweal, west of Bryher, on her second voyage, in March 1861. The crew scrambled along her spars onto the rocks and were saved by the men of Bryher. She was refloated but broke up on a beach on Bryher later in the same month. Much was saved apart from the trail boards; the capstan and billet-head (see nos. 21,55) came to 'Valhalla' and timber from her was used to panel the state rooms of Tresco Abbey. Salvage money — £100 — received by the Bryher Islanders paid for a new pilot gig, *Golden Eagle*, which when built in 1870 cost £1 per foot, masts, sails and oars extra. The *Golden Eagle* survives and regularly takes part in the summer gig races.

***AWARD:*** Wooden ship of 846 tons **R**: Liverpool
**B**: Gilmour, Quebec, 1859. **D**: —
**O**: Rankin & Co **M**: Watts
**V**: Liverpool to New Orleans **C**: Wheat **W**: 16.3.1861

2.

## SALMON 2

Some years later a much smaller Quebec-built vessel, the *Salmon*, was driven onto the Mare Ledges off the south end of Tresco, in a south-westerly gale. She was converted to schooner rig in 1869, having been built a brigantine, and was sheltering off St Mary's on passage for South Africa when her anchor cable parted. All her crew were saved, as well as her figurehead.

***SALMON:*** Wooden schooner of 178 tons **R**: Scilly
**B**: Laprise, Quebec, 1859 **D**: 96.6×23.0×12.0
**O**: James Phillips, St Mary's, Scilly **M**: Jenkins, Scilly
**V**: London to East London **C**: General cargo **W**: 15.1.1871

## INDIPENDENZA 3

A small white bust of a young lady from a Genoese barque lost in 1881. On passage from Valparaiso with guano, hooves and horn, a crew of 14 and a pilot on board, she encountered dense fog and was thought to be 15 miles south-west of the islands. This estimate proved wrong when she struck four times on the Crims, north of the Bishop Rock. She was pulled off, only to drift back and remained lodged for about five minutes while the water rose to about six feet in her hold. She floated off and her master tried to bring her into St Mary's; she drifted and was finally wrecked on the Barrel of Butter, the western point of that island. Almost all her cargo was lost and St Mary's Pool was reported to be "thick with horns" (see also no. 16).

***INDIPENDENZA**:* Wooden barque of 837 tons **R:** Recco
**B:** Peragallo, Sestri Ponente, 1875 **D:** 164.7×33.6×22.7
**O:** G Marano, of Recco **M:** Fillipo Caffarena
**V:** Valparaiso to Rotterdam **C:** As above **W:** 20.9.1881

3.

5.

## OREGON 4

All that remains of this vessel is her nameboard, for no such wreck is recorded on the Isles of Scilly or the nearby coast. An *Oregon* is listed as being driven ashore under Picklecombe Fort, Plymouth, in 1867 and after being pulled off was reported as being "stripped". This could have been the source of the piece.

## SERICA 5

The figurehead of a woman wearing a small crown, from a schooner-rigged screw steamer, the *Serica* of London.

Outward bound from Cardiff with coal, the *Serica* was damaged in a gale off Hartland Point on 17th November 1893. On two occasions the master was washed overboard and washed back again! She made Scilly with her hatch tarpaulins ripped, the main cabin flooded, her pumps choked and a considerable list. She was able to leave again on the 24th but rounding the south-west of St Mary's, off the Woolpack, she struck a rock and had to be run ashore, where she was abandoned. This hazard, nearer the surface than indicated on charts of the time, has since been known as Serica Rock. Charlotte Dorrien-Smith remembered taking part in the salvage; "The figurehead is in the Valhalla" she wrote. "We went down in the gig *Normandy* and cut it off".

***SERICA**:* Screw steamer/schooner rig, 2652 tons **R:** London
**B:** Sunderland Shipbuilding Co, 1889 **D:** 321.5×40.2×19.0
**O:** R Gordon & Co **M:** Sidney Smith
**V:** Cardiff to Port Said **C:** Coal **W:** 24.11.1893

## 'GOLDEN LION' 6

Gilded figurehead of a lion, possibly from a vessel called *Lion*, although nothing is known of a wreck; there is a tradition that this head came from a wreck off Land's End.

## *PRIMOS* 7

A fine life-size, white-painted female figurehead, with gilded decoration, from a Spanish barque which struck the Seven Stones in 1871.

In heavy weather and about dawn, she hit these notorious rocks between the Islands and Land's End, where almost a hundred years later the super-tanker *Torrey Canyon* was to be wrecked. One of her boats drifted away and another capsized

Wreck of the *Serica*, 1893.

6.

7.

with the master and four crew before the *Primos* foundered, barely 12 minutes after striking. All eleven crew were drowned except for Vincenzo Defilice who had a remarkable escape. After swimming for some hours he found a floating hen coop, onto which he climbed and kept afloat for a further hour. He then saw the ship's figurehead, to which he was able to cling for several hours before one of the *Primos'* own boats drifted by; in this he rowed himself to English Island Neck where he was rescued by Scilly pilots. By these strange methods he had travelled a distance of at least 8½ miles in the open sea. According to tradition, Defilice knew he would be saved because of the serene expression on the face of the figurehead. The figurehead washed ashore on St Martin's.

***PRIMOS*:** Iron barque of 466 tons
**B:** Oswald of Sunderland, 1869
**O:** De Anduza
**V:** Havana to Falmouth and Greenock **C:** Sugar
**R:** Bilbao
**D:** 155.6×27.2×16.0
**M:** Anduza
**W:** 24.6 1871

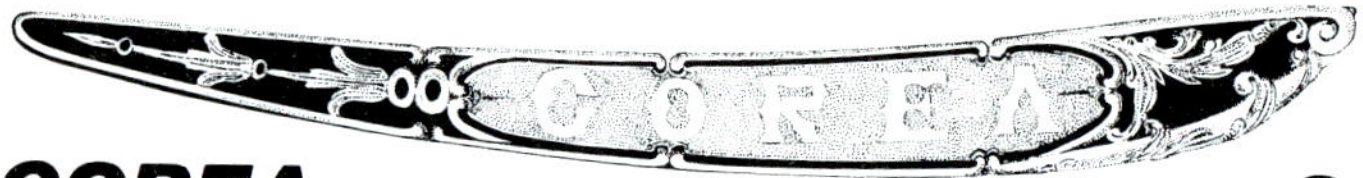


## COREA 8

Traditionally this nameboard comes from a Portuguese vessel wrecked in 1890 while bound from Cardiff to Oporto with coal. However, Lloyds neither reported such a wreck nor has any record of the ship been found. It may be that the board actually comes from a British steamer of 1321 tons, built in 1890 and owned by Stephens, Mawson and Goss of Newport, South Wales. On 18th February 1892 while bound from Cardiff to Genoa she collided with the Norwegian steamer *Norden* off southern Portugal and went ashore near Aljezur; no lives were lost. A British salvage vessel from Cadiz surveyed the wreck and reported it a total loss. If this is the right ship it is more likely that the board was brought home as a souvenir rather than floating back but even this is possible.

## RIVER LUNE 9

A finely carved female figurehead from the iron barque *River Lune.* Captain George West's estimated position was 10 to 15 miles west of the Bishop Rock when, through thick fog, the lookout sighted rocks all around them. In attempting to come about she struck the Brothers Rocks and started to go down. The crew abandoned ship but later were able to return and collect their personal belongings. Although only 11 years old, her wreck fetched no more than £55 and her figurehead was saved for 'Valhalla'

***RIVER LUNE:*** Iron barque of 1172 tons
**B**: Schlesinger, Wallsend, 1868
**O**: John Hargrove & Co
**V**: Lorient to Ardrossan
**C**: In ballast
**R**: Liverpool
**D**: 216.0×35.6×22.2
**M**: George West
**W**: 27.7.1879

9.

*River Lune* on the Brothers Rocks, 1879.

## LOFARO 10

Dark green painted and gilded billet-head from a Neapolitan barque which, in February 1902, went down with all hands on rocks in St Martin's Bay, in a strong north-easterly wind. *Lofaro* was first sighted by a St Martin's coastguard but he left for his tea before there were signs that she was in trouble. When this became evident, the Round Island lighthouse keeper fired distress rockets to call the lifeboat from St Mary's; the local gig *Emperor* tried to give assistance but was prevented from rounding St Martin's Head by the high seas. After *Lofaro* went onto Merrick Rock the crew were seen swimming for the shore; all were lost and the lifeboat, now searching by lantern light in complete darkness, could only find wreckage. The next morning *Lofaro's* keel, with stem and stern posts attached, had been washed up; also three bodies and a chest, which contained the master's gold watch and the ship's papers, by which she was identified.

***LOFARO:*** *Wooden barque of 721 tons* — **R**: Naples
**B**: F Sirello, Savona, 1876 — **D**: 159.8×30.1×21.0
**O**: Francesco Lofaro di Pietro, Torre del Greco — **M**: A Ruffo
**V**: Hamburg to Cardiff — **C**: In ballast — **W**: 2.2.1902

---

## STERNBOARD with cornucopia 11

The fine standard of carving of the intertwined cornucopia indicates a vessel of quality but from which ship and how the board arrived at 'Valhalla' is unknown.

10.

11.

# BOSPHORUS 12

The *Bosphorus,* known locally as the "Old Turk" was built and owned in the Islands. Originally trading to the Mediterranean in the 1840s, she could well have been carrying salted pilchards from fish cellars then recently established. She was then owned jointly by William Tremenheere Johns and her master.

According to her registration records her figurehead was removed in 1861, presumably at the time of her sale; her new owners registered her at Maldon, Essex, from 1865. She then worked on the East Coast, eventually going ashore without loss of life in the small hours of an October night in 1880, a mile south of Scarborough.

12.

***BOSPHORUS**:* Wooden schooner of 199 tons **R**: Scilly, then Maldon
**B**: William Mumford, St Mary's, 1840 **D**: 89.0×22.3×14.3
**O**: H Clark, Maldon **M**: Mulley
**V**: Portsmouth to the Tyne **C**: In ballast **W**: 29.10.1880

# CITÉ DE VERDUN 13

A lifebuoy from a French steam trawler with a crew of 30 which went onto Rosevear, shortly after the lookouts had briefly glimpsed the Bishop Rock light through a heavy snowstorm. The crew built a shelter on the islet before sending up distress flares. After just three-quarters of an hour all were on board the St Mary's lifeboat, the crew of which later received awards from the French government. The nameboard of the *Cité de Verdun* was also saved and is now in the Atlantic Hotel, St Mary's.

***CITÉ DE VERDUN**:* Steam trawler of 214 tons **R**: Boulogne
**B**: de Groot & van Vliet, Slikkerveer, 1916 **D**: 115.5×22.2×11.0
**O**: J B Bourgain **M**: —
**V**: Fishing **C**: — **W**: 22.3.1925

# BANDOENG 14

A lifebuoy from one of the six Dutch steamers, which (with one Norwegian) were sunk by a German submarine one day early in 1917, some 30 miles north-west of the Bishop Rock light. Some of their survivors, in two boats, were spotted from the lighthouse and as a result the St Agnes lifeboat was launched. After a wide search it found one more boat. This brought the total of survivors to 47, the incident being of note as the ships, all from neutral countries, were fired on without warning. Apparently none of the *Bandoeng's* crew were lost.

***BANDOENG**:* Screw steamer of 5851 tons **R**: Rotterdam
**B**: Bonn & Mees, Rotterdam, 1910 **D**: 393.6×51.3×26.2
**O**: Rotterdamsche Lloyd **M**: van der Eem (?)
**V**: Batavia (Djakarta) to Falmouth and Rotterdam **C**: Java products **W**: Torpedoed 22.2.1917

# THOMAS W LAWSON 15

A lifebuoy from the largest sailing vessel ever built, the seven-masted *Thomas W. Lawson,* which ended her short career off Annett in 1907. Built in the steam age, in an attempt to show that sail could still be competitive, she was designed with fore-and-aft rig and donkey engines at each mast to raise her enormous areas of canvas — over 40,000 square feet in all, or almost an acre. She had a crew of 18 when a similar sized steamer would have required anything up to 50.

395 ft long overall, she was carrying 2,225,000 gallons of paraffin oil, when following a rough Atlantic crossing she was brought to anchor in Broad Sound, only 6 of her sails remaining serviceable. Here it was hoped she could ride out the storm and when the St Agnes lifeboat reached her the Captain would only agree to taking a pilot on board. Charlotte Dorrien-Smith remembered; "The Captain hoisted no signals of distress and said he did not consider himself in any danger. With his tackle he could have ridden out any storm on the American coast, but alas, not here". During the following night, as the gale reached 90 mph, the ship's cables parted and she was driven helplessly onto Shag Rock, west of Annett, capsizing and throwing her crew into the sea. Next morning, floating wreckage suggested to those watching on St Agnes what must have occurred and the St Agnes gig *Slippen* set out in high seas to search for survivors. Those who could be seen on Annett were dead by the time the weather made a landing possible but later a seaman from London was found on the island; he subsequently died. *Slippen* continued to search and on Hellweathers the master and engineer were found. Frederick Cook Hicks, son of the pilot who had been lost, swam a line through the surf to make an heroic rescue but all the remaining crew died.

***THOMAS W LAWSON:*** 7-masted steel schooner of 5218 tons
**B**: Fore River Eng. Co, Quincy, Mass., 1902
**O**: Coastwise Transportation Co.
**V**: Philadelphia to London **C**: Paraffin oil
**R**: Boston, Mass.
**D**: 375.6×50.0×22.9
**M**: George Dow
**W**: 14.12.1907

The *Thomas W Lawson.*

## *INDIPENDENZA* 16

The nameboard from a large Genoese barque, the figurehead also being in the collection (see no. 3).

---

## MALE HALF-FIGURE 17

Figurehead of a man dressed in late Georgian frock coat and cravat, perhaps as late as the 1840s. The origins of this item are unrecorded.

---

## *MAIPU* 18

A small shield from the centre of the decorated stern of the Liverpool barque *Maipu,* lost in July 1879. She had called at Cork and was approaching the Islands in fog, when Captain Wheeler heard breakers ahead. Nothing could be heard by forward lookouts above the wind drumming the foresail until land was

17.

18.

actually sighted; then, despite attempts to come about, she struck hard on rocks in Hell Bay, Bryher, going down slowly by the head. Having been declared a total loss, she was sold to a group on the Island for £7 but on 18th August she broke up, the shield and figurehead surviving, although the whereabouts of the latter is not known. A few hours after the *Maipu* struck, the *River Lune* (see no. 9) went down, a victim of the same fog. Maipu is the name of several South American towns, this ship probably being so-called after one in Chile.

***MAIPU:*** Iron barque of 594 tons
**B**: Laird, Birkenhead, 1865
**O**: Brooke & Worthington
**V**: Iquique to Hamburg
**C**: Saltpetre
**R**: Liverpool
**D**: 166.6×28.3×18.3
**M**: Thomas Wheeler
**W**: 27.7.1879

*Maipu,* wrecked in Hell Bay, Bryher, 1879.

## STERNBOARD 19

Ten foot wide sternboard with white and gilded decoration on blue, from an unknown vessel.

19.

No. 20; side boards of the *Sophie* with *Award* billet-head, no. 21, below.

## *SOPHIE* 20

Pair of fine sideboards from the billet-head of the *Sophie,* painted black with gilded decoration. When this dismasted Norwegian barque was first seen and then boarded by a gig crew it appeared to be another *Marie Celeste* mystery. All was in order — table laid, warm food on the stove and the clock still wound — but a well-fed dog was the only life aboard. Two gigs, the St Mary's lifeboat and the Scilly packet *Lady of the Isles* brought her 2½ miles to anchor off New Grimsby. Five days later the mystery was solved when her crew arrived at Gibraltar on the British steamer *Glenmore.* It appeared that although she had been replanked over her original planking, the 39-year-old *Sophie* was thought to be breaking up; so the crew had abandoned her. However she was not totally abandoned, so the owners claimed, in the salvage proceedings, since the dog had remained on board! Algernon Dorrien-Smith bought her hulk for £250, using much of her timber on the Tresco estate and her cargo of coal to heat his greenhouses. See illustration on back cover.

***SOPHIE*:** Wooden barque of 549 tons
**B**: Helsingfors (Helsinki), 1857
**O**: Actielskabet 'Sophie' (J Bjorge).
**V**: Cardiff to Frederickstad **C**: Anthracite
**R**: Frederickstad
**D**: 135.2×33.7×18.2
**M**: C Bjorge
**W**: Found abandoned 15.12.1896

## *AWARD* 21

Black and gilded billet-head from the *Award* (see no 1).

21.

## *INTREPID* 22

Nothing is recorded of a wreck of this name on the Isles of Scilly. It is therefore possible that this nameboard comes from a Sunderland brig which was wrecked off Pendeen, north of Land's End, in 1847. It may have become detached and drifted over to the Islands, or Augustus Smith could have acquired it for his collection while on the mainland.

---

## *ALESSANDRO IL GRANDE* 23

From a brig of Venice (then an Austrian city) this bust in military uniform is a portrait of Tsar Alexander I of Russia (reigned 1801–25). While sheltering in St Mary's Roads on New Year's Day, 1851, her anchor cables parted and she was driven onto the Mare Ledges off the south of Tresco at 10pm. She was a total loss, although there was an opportunity to recover the ship's stores and there were no casualties. These same rocks were later to claim the *Salmon* (see no. 2).

***ALESSANDRO IL GRANDE:*** Wooden brig of 289 tons
**B:** ? 1801–25
**O:** —
**R:** Venice
**D:** —
**M:** Santo Amadeo Gavaquin
**V:** Galway to Cardiff
**C:** In ballast
**W:** 1.1.1851

*23.*

*25.*

---

## *FLORA* 24

This nameboard reputedly came from a wreck on Guthers Rock in 1853 but the recorded details would appear to relate to the loss there of the *Sultana* of Hamburg rather than the *Flora.* There is no recorded wreck of a *Flora* in the Islands and identification is not helped by its being such a popular name, particularly in Scandinavia. A number of *Flora's* can be found in most 19th century editions of *Lloyd's Register of Shipping.*

## FEMALE FIGURE 25

This example and that from *Bernardo* (no. 53) show a variation on the usual form in which a figure is designed to sit within a modified billet-bead. In this case the figure is of a red-haired girl dressed in blue but nothing is known of its origin.

---

## FALKLAND 26

The damaged female head from a four-masted barque which, quite literally, struck the Bishop Rock lighthouse early one summer evening in 1901. She was 135 days out from Tacoma, Washington State, with wheat when she carried broadside onto the Rock in a south-westerly gale, her mainyard striking the lighthouse tower. She drifted for half-a-mile before she went over on her beam ends. Her port-side boat was launched and 25 crew with the master's wife and child got away safely. The master, mate, steward and three seamen were drowned as the *Falkland* suddenly lost buoyancy after her charthouse roof was blown off by the pressure of air inside her. They had unsuccessfully been attempting to launch the starboard boat which at first jammed and then fell out of its stowage. The 27 survivors and their boat were then taken in by the St Agnes lifeboat, *James and Caroline*.

***FALKLAND:*** 4-masted iron barque of 2867 tons
**B**: W H Potter & Sons, Liverpool, 1889
**O**: "Ship Falkland" Co Ltd (Macvicar, Marshall & Co)
**V**: Tacoma to Falmouth **C**: Wheat
**R**: Liverpool
**D**: 317.8×45.3×24.9
**M**: G S Gracie
**W**: 22.6.1901

*26.*

## FRIAR TUCK 27

Over five hundred sailing vessels were sheltering from strong winds in St. Mary's Roads at the end of November 1863. Six of these did not survive the hurricane which followed and amongst them was the Liverpool tea-clipper *Friar Tuck.* On 2nd December she parted her cables and as she went onto Newford Island, in St Mary's Pool, Captain Fordyce ordered her masts to be cut away. A rocket line from the shore saved her crew of 22. Three small shiploads of tea, sails, spars and some stores were taken to London but the Islanders managed to "acquire" large quantities of tea, despite the efforts of coastguards and preventive men. A lasting monument to the *Friar Tuck,* apart from her figurehead, are the Chinese geese on Tresco which are descendants of those which came ashore from the wreck. The ship had been a good investment for her owners with profits of £12,389 over six years. It was the prospect of such returns which induced owners to spend money on fine figureheads and other decoration for their vessels.

***FRIAR TUCK:*** Wooden ship of 662 tons
**B**: A Hall & Co, Aberdeen, 1856
**O**: J Beazley, Liverpool
**V**: Foochow to London **C**: Tea
**R**: Liverpool
**D**: 193.2×31.0×17.0
**M**: Fordyce
**W**: 2.12.1863

*27.*

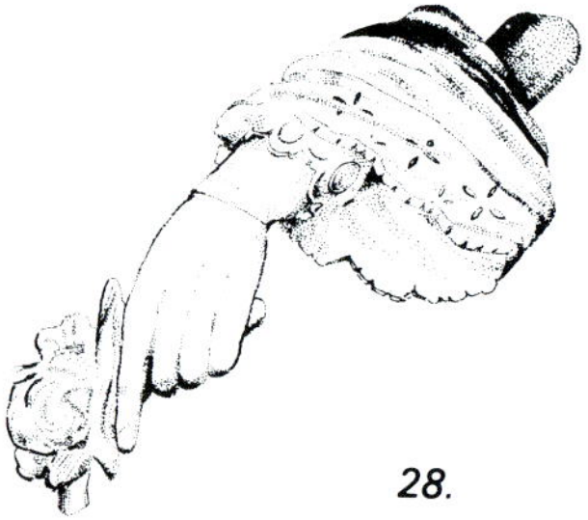

28.

29.

## FEMALE HAND with flowers 28

Female figureheads often hold a flower or nosegay to their breast (see nos. 25,49 for example). This is presumably the source of this fragment.

## SPANISH LADY 29

A full-length figurehead of a lady, traditionally thought to be Spanish. There is no record of the origins of the piece.

## *COLOSSUS* 30

One of the earlier items in the collection is the decorated late 18th century sternboard from HMS *Colossus.* Her wreck in 1798 was certainly a major disaster but is now chiefly remembered for the extraordinary cargo on board when she went down. After nearly two years' service in the Mediterranean, including action at the Battle of Cape St Vincent, 1797, *Colossus* was returning home barely seaworthy. She was also overcrowded with wounded from the Battle of the Nile in August 1798, as well as her usual complement. In addition she carried a large collection of Etruscan and Roman vases, statuary, paintings and other treasures belonging to Sir William Hamilton, the British Envoy at Naples and husband of the celebrated Emma, Nelson's *inamorata.*

*Colossus* arrived in charge of a convoy in St Mary's Roads, to shelter from a north-easter on 7th December. On the 10th the wind went round to south-east and increased to a gale. The main bower cable parted and other anchors failed to hold on the sandy

31.

30.

bottom. By evening she had struck rocks to the south of Samson and next morning she had to be abandoned; she began to break up the following night.

Much was salvaged, including, to his despair, only two-thirds of Hamilton's collection and, to his fury, the body of Admiral Lord Shuldham (who had died abroad) coming home pickled in a lead casket. Sir William commented that "it can be of no use but to the worms, but my collection would have given information to the most learned".

Some of the guns from *Colossus* were raised in 1852 and put into service on the Garrison, St Mary's, where they can still be seen. In more recent years further fragments of pottery from the Hamilton collection have been recovered by divers.

***COLOSSUS**:* 3rd rate ship of the line, 74 guns, 1717 tons (old measurement)
**B**: Cleveley, Gravesend, 1787
**D**: 172.3 (gun deck) ×48×20.9
**Captain:** George Murray
**V**: Inward bound from Lisbon
**W**: 10.12.1798

## 'GOLDEN EAGLE' 31

Little is known about this very skilfully carved and gilded eagle, with a snake held in its beak. It is supposed to be a Mexican eagle from a French wreck of before 1850.

## ANCHOR 32

This 'Spanish' anchor was found by divers in St Mary's Roads.

## ANCHOR 33

This anchor was probably found and raised during the search which followed the sinking of the gig *Hound*. She was returning with members of the St Agnes Cricket Club, following a match on Tresco, in July 1875 and four of those on board were drowned. The origins of this anchor and of no. 32 are unknown.

Parts of an Admiralty pattern anchor, with folding stock.

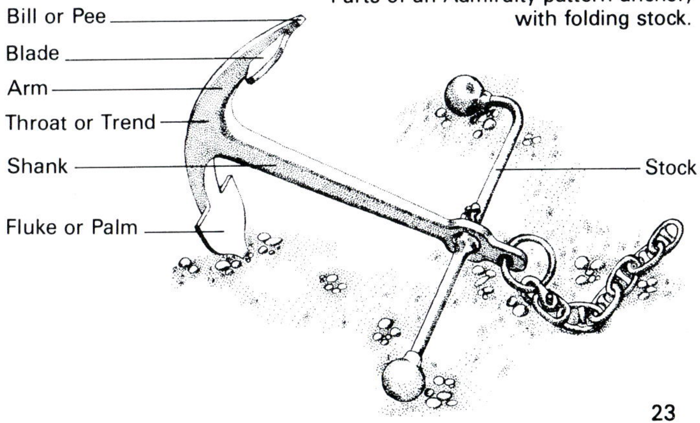

## *PALINURUS* 34

A full-sized figure in formal dress of c. 1830 and holding a sword above his head, from the *Palinurus* which went onto the Lion Rock, off the north of St Martin's, while inward bound from Demerara in 1848. All her crew of 17 were drowned, eventually washed ashore and buried on St Mary's. The first alarm was raised by cattle, frightened out of their field by the noise of the vessel's sails flapping and tearing in the wind. Local people managed to save some of her cargo, 14 hogsheads and 71 puncheons of spirits and 9 quarter-casks of rum being brought ashore. Palinurus is the name of the helmsman of Achilles in Homer's *Iliad.*

'Polinarus', the traditional local name for the piece, is understandable but incorrect.

***PALINURUS:*** Wooden barque of 300 tons
**B**: Whitby, 1833
**O**: Embleton
**V**: Demerara to London
**C**: Rum and other spirits
**R**: London
**D**: —
**M**: Allen or Gorl
**W**: 27.12.1848

34.

36.



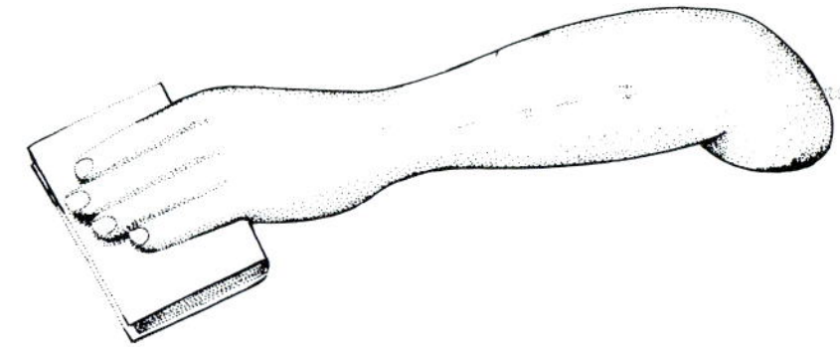

## FEMALE HAND with book 35

Like no. 28 but holding a small book, this is presumably from a figurehead but nothing more is known of it.

---

## FEMALE FIGURE 36

A full-length female figurehead, dressed in a 'shepherdess' or pastoral style but about which nothing is known.

---

## GILDED CORNUCOPIA 37

A small item which may well be part of the stern decoration of a vessel.

37.

## 'DOLPHIN' 38

This fish figurehead, traditionally known as the "Dolphin", may well come from a vessel of that name, of which there were many in the last century. Again, nothing has been recorded and no *Dolphin* is known to have been wrecked on the Scillies.

38.

## ROMAN SOLDIER FIGURE 39

Another male figurehead about which nothing is known. Its costume suggests it came from a vessel whose name had some association with ancient Rome.

---

## *MARY HAY* 40

Elegant female half-figure supported on a black and gilded scroll from the barque *Mary Hay.* Bound from Jamaica with a mixed cargo including rum and sugar, she was approaching Broad Sound with a Scilly pilot on board. Just after he went below to take a meal, rather than eating on deck, she hit Steeple Rock and began to make water. She anchored near Samson, pumping continuously but to no avail since several hours later she turned over with a sudden lurch.

All hands were saved, being on deck or in the boats alongside at the time. Next day rum, limejuice and over a thousand bags of pimentos were saved, with clothing, stores and some gear. The sugar was ruined but the rest of the cargo was included in the sale of the wreck for £72, four days later. In calmer weather she was refloated and broken up alongside St Mary's pier.

*MARY HAY:* Wooden barque of 258 tons
**B:** Peterhead, 1837
**O:** Volum & Co
**V:** Jamaica to London
**R:** London
**D:** —
**M:** Hogg
**W:** 13.4.1852
**C:** As above, also ebony, coconuts, logwood and fustic (woods from which dye is extracted)

39.

40.

## VOLUNTEER 41

This small half-kneeling figure of a Volunteer with his rifle is from an old coasting ketch that supplied the Islands with coal. She had been built and owned in Aberystwyth and in 1908 came to Scilly, already 47 years old. Three years later she foundered on Culver Sands in the Bristol Channel and her owners then had the figurehead brought back to Tresco for 'Valhalla'.

***VOLUNTEER**:* Wooden ketch of 65 tons
**B**: Edward James, Aberystwyth, 1861
**O**: Stephen and Rosamund Helen Jenkins
**V**: S Wales to Scilly (?) **C**: Coal
**R**: Scilly
**D**: 71.1×18.6×8.2
**M**: W Parkin (?)
**W**: 26.1.1911

## RICHARD BROWN 42

The origin of this small nameboard is unknown as no *Richard Brown* seems to have been lost around Scilly or the west of England. A small Glasgow brig of the name was wrecked near Calais in 1861 but it is hard to see how its nameboard could have reached Tresco.

---

## FEMALE HALF-FIGURE 43

Another rather simple item about which nothing is known.

*41.*

*43.*

*44.*

*45.*

## ROSHERVILLE 44

A finely carved half-figure of a gentleman wearing a cravat from the *Rosherville* of London, said to be a former French prize. She was at anchor in St Mary's Roads in 1855 and discharging some of her cargo, having arrived with her pumps choked, when she caught fire. When her cable burnt through she drifted and was beached at Pendrathen, near Bar Point, the northern tip of St Mary's. The tide extinguished the flames and by next day just a gutted hulk remained.

***ROSHERVILLE:*** Wooden brig or brigantine
**B:** —
**O:** —
**V:** London to Rio de Janeiro
**R:** London
**D:** -
**M:** Brabyn
**W:** 3.3.1855
**C:** Rice, beer, wine, brandy

---

## JANE OWEN 45

This pretty little female half-figure in a blue dress is from a small Welsh schooner and may be a portrait figurehead.

She was on her way to Devonport in 1889 with a cargo of slates, when she was wrecked on the Queen's Ledge. She was later brought onto the beach by the farm buildings on Tresco to be broken up.

***JANE OWEN:*** Wooden schooner of 76 tons
**B:** Evans, Pwllheli, 1860
**O:** R Jenkins, Aberdovey
**V:** Aberdovey to Devonport
**C:** Welsh slates
**R:** Caernarvon
**D:** 68.2×19.7×9.3
**M:** R Jenkins
**W:** 3.3.1889

---

## 'BOREAS' 46

According to tradition this elaborate black and gilded stern decoration comes from a 17th century French East Indiaman wrecked on Annett and is said to be the work of the noted French carver Pierre Puget, who died in 1694. It has not yet been possible to prove this but, if true, the piece would be the earliest in the collection. The way it is mounted, as shown here, will in due course be slightly altered as the small cloud pieces should trail behind the figures. These, which are somewhat irreverently nicknamed 'the Puffers', may have been quarter gallery decorations; the thunderbolts are probably a sternboard. Boreas, the Greek god of the north wind, is the name traditionally ascribed to the ship.

46.

# SCHILLER 47

A pair of brass signal guns from the worst passenger ship disaster in the Islands, when (by the official figures) 335 lives were lost, in 1875.

The SS *Schiller* of Hamburg was returning from New York and was due to land 22 of her passengers at Plymouth. Approaching the Islands in dense fog, Captain Thomas reduced speed and enlisted some of the male passengers as additional lookouts. Shortly before 10pm, however, the ship struck the Retarrier Ledge; she managed to pull herself off but then, following three huge waves, struck again broadside on. Only one shot from her signal guns was heard on the Islands and this was thought to be no more than a vessel notifying her arrival off Scilly.

The horrifying fate of the passengers and crew — women and children washed overboard in the darkness, lifeboats smashed to pieces in the heavy seas — is all told in detail in Richard Larn's *Cornish Shipwrecks; The Isles of Scilly* (1971). Only two of the the eight lifeboats got clear and when rescue arrived the next morning it was found that very few people had survived the night. The two lifeboats landed on Tresco with 26 of the 37 still alive from the crew of 118 and 254 passengers.

Most of the 250 bags of Australian and New Zealand mails were washed up on Samson or, with other cargo, came ashore around the Cornish coast for weeks after. But the *Schiller* also carried quantities of gold and other valuables and as the weather eased divers went down to search the wreck. A year later they had recovered £57,000 of the £60,000-worth of $20 gold coin which she carried, as well as some cargo and passengers' valuables. The bodies landed on St Mary's had to be buried, this proving no small problem since mass graves had to be dug and blasted out of the rock. See illustration on page 6.

The *Schiller*'s bridge was salvaged and built into Tresco Abbey, as a link between the house and conservatory.

***SCHILLER:*** Iron passenger screw steamer of 3421 tons
**R:** Hamburg
**B:** Napiers of Glasgow for Alexander Stephens, 1873
**D:** 380.5×40.1×24.4
**O:** German Transatlantic Steam Navigation Co
**M:** Thomas
**V:** New York, Plymouth, Hamburg
**W:** 7.5.1875
**C:** Passengers, specie, general cargo

*47.*

The SS *Schiller*; from an engraving in the *Illustrated London News* at the time of her loss, 1875.

## *TURQUOISE* 48

The transom of a lifeboat from one of two coasters belonging to William Robertson of Glasgow, which were converted to fleet messengers in the First World War. They were on their way to the Dardanelles in 1915 when sunk by gunfire from the German submarine U28. *Nugget* sank off Porth Hellick on St Mary's before she could be beached, while *Turquoise* went down well out to sea. Although U28 fired on the crews while in their boats, the survivors were brought into St Mary's by the naval patrol boat, *Anthony Hope*.

***TURQUOISE***: Screw steamer of 486 tons
**B**: J Shearer and Sons, Glasgow, 1893
**O**: William Robertson
**V**: — **C**: —
**R**: Glasgow
**D**: 165.2×26.1×11.1
**M**: J McGougan (?)
**W**: 31.7.1915

## 'PURITAN LADY' 49

Although known from its appearance as the 'Puritan Lady' nothing is recorded about this figurehead's origins.

49.

48.

## 'CHIEFTAIN' 50

A fine figurehead in Highland dress, previously thought to have come from a vessel named *Chieftain*, wrecked on Hard Lewis in 1856. No records exist of such a wreck and indeed no likely vessel of that name was registered at the time. Exactly 10 years later the *Gilmore* of Southampton was wrecked on Hard Lewis, the figurehead being equally appropriate to a ship of that name. At present though, it is impossible to provide a firm identification.

50.

51.

52.

53.

## FEMALE HALF-FIGURE 51

Small female head and torso from an unrecorded wreck.

---

## *ELIZA* 52

A brightly decorated scroll-head with flowers and bunches of grapes, which by tradition comes from a vessel stationed as a coal hulk off Nut Rock, south of Tresco. According to Charlotte Dorrien-Smith it was wrecked in 1867, but nothing further is known of its origins.

---

## *BERNARDO* 53

The Italian barque *Bernardo* was blown ashore on Annett in 1888 after her sails had been carried away by a north-westerly gale. The crew managed to launch a boat but this was overturned, drowning all eleven seamen. Only Captain Dapelo was left on the *Bernardo* and as his ship began to break up he had to swim. The sole survivor, he reached the Old Woman Rock where he was able to hold on until rescued by a fishing boat. This is the second figure in the collection which is incorporated into the design of the billet-head (see also no. 25); it appears to represent St Bernard of Clairvaux, holding a pastoral staff, although this identification is not intirely convincing.

***BERNARDO**:* Wooden barque of 701 tons
**B**: A Rollo, Varazze, 1876
**O**: G B Degregori, Camogli
**V**: Alicante to Cardiff
**C**: In ballast
**R**: Genoa
**D**: 152.8×30.5×21.0
**M**: Dapelo
**W**: 11.3.1888

## SAN JOSEF — 54

This simple wooden wedge is the elevating quoin from a 32-pounder gun (similar to that on the *Association* gun, no. 58). It was found in the Woolpack Battery, St Mary's, and is thought to come from the great Spanish three-decker of 112 guns, brilliantly captured by Nelson at the Battle of Cape St Vincent in 1797. The quoin may have arrived indirectly from the *Colossus* (see no. 30), which also took part in the action. More probably, it came later from Devonport where the *San Josef* spent her last years and where she was broken up in 1849. Her bell and a table made from her timber are in the National Maritime Museum at Greenwich.

## AWARD — 55

Capstan from the *Award*; for details of this vessel see no. 1.

55.

57.

English version of the *San Josef*'s name on the head of no. 54.

## ROSA TACCHINI — 56

This small female figurehead has been kept in its unrestored condition as an example of the state some items were in, washed up after some time in the sea and before skilled restoration was begun. Little is known about the *Rosa Tacchini* but while sheltering from a south-westerly gale in 1872, her anchor cables parted. She was driven onto the Paper Ledges, south of Tresco and no more than three-quarters of a mile from 'Valhalla'.

She became a total wreck, having struck twice before settling on the rocks. See illustration on page 9.

***ROSA TACCHINI:*** Wooden barque, probably Italian

**B:** —
**O:** —
**V:** Buenos Aires to Antwerp
**R:** —
**D:** —
**M:** Abbate
**W:** 22.11.1872
**C:** Hides, horns, hooves, tallow, wool

## WHITE PLAQUE — 57

A small white plaque with rose, thistle and shamrock, which could have been a decorative panel on a vessel but may more likely be a carver's sample or the work of an apprentice. The plants are respectively symbols of England, Scotland and Ireland.

58.

## ASSOCIATION 58

The wreck of Sir Cloudesley Shovell's fleet is a well-known maritime disaster in which 2,000 officers and men were drowned. Of the 15 ships of the line, five frigates and a yacht under Shovell's command, the *Romney, Association, Eagle* and *Firebrand* all went down on the evening of 22nd October 1707. Returning through stormy weather from a successful commission in the Mediterranean the fleet's position was estimated to be much further south of the Islands. Sir Cloudesley's *Association* struck the Gilstone Ledges, sinking immediately, while the *Eagle, Firebrand* and *Romney* all struck and were lost nearby. It was reported that there were only 26 survivors from the four ships and they did not include Sir Cloudesley; thirty years later, a local woman confessed on her deathbed that she had found him washed up, barely alive, and had 'finished him off' for the sake of the emerald ring on his finger. There are, however, good reasons for doubting this story.

The *Association* in particular had been carrying considerable treasure and there was activity around the wreck for some time. Much material was rescued by the Islanders while part of the great ship remained above water and an official salvage operation was mounted in 1709. The wreck was located again in the 19th century; then the site was forgotten until Royal Navy divers rediscovered it in 1967. After this many cannon and a large quantity of coin and other artifacts were found and raised. The bronze gun at 'Valhalla' was brought up in 1970 and sold by auction in Penzance, with other material from the wreck. It is a French 17th century naval piece, probably made during the reign of Louix XIV (reigned 1643–1715). It bears the arms of France and the royal 'L' cypher and was captured at Vigo in 1702 or Toulon in 1707. Its shot weight was 18 pounds and it was probably being carried home as a prize rather than as one of the ship's guns. The carriage is modern.

In the long term the *Association* disaster had two good effects. It intensified 18th century work to find a reliable means of establishing longitude at sea — eventually achieved with the invention of the marine chronometer. In our own time some controversial aspects of the salvage and sale of material from the *Association* and her consorts helped lead to the 1973 Act for the Protection of Historic Wrecks. Shovell is buried in Westminster Abbey.

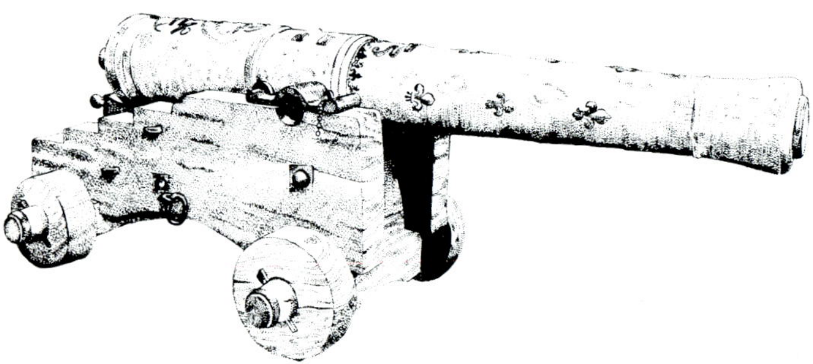

***ASSOCIATION:*** 2nd rate ship of the line, 90 guns, 1459 tons (old measurement)
**B:** Portsmouth Dockyard, 1697
**V:** Inward bound from Gibraltar

**D:** 165 (gun deck) × 45.4×18.3
**Captain:** Samuel Whitaker
**W:** 22.10.1707